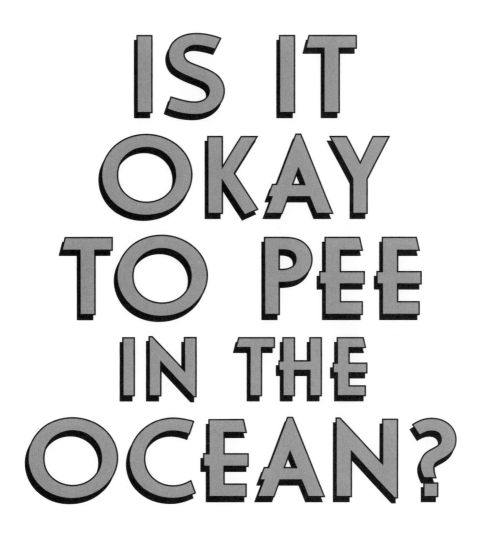

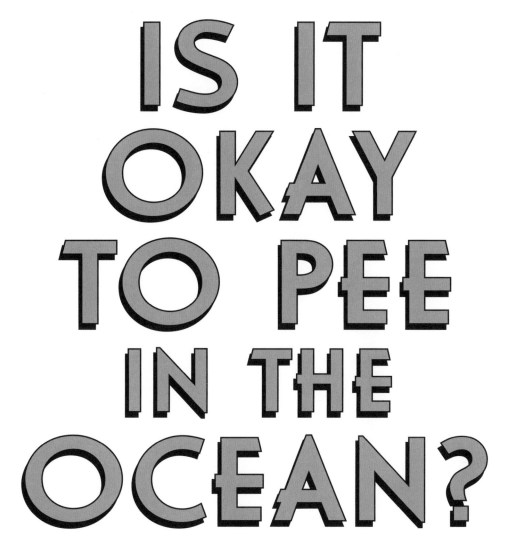

IS IT OKAY TO PEE IN THE OCEAN?

THE FASCINATING SCIENCE OF OUR WASTE AND OUR WORLD

ELLA SCHWARTZ
illustrated by LILY WILLIAMS

BLOOMSBURY
CHILDREN'S BOOKS
NEW YORK LONDON OXFORD NEW DELHI SYDNEY

BLOOMSBURY CHILDREN'S BOOKS
Bloomsbury Publishing Inc., part of Bloomsbury Publishing Plc
1385 Broadway, New York, NY 10018

BLOOMSBURY, BLOOMSBURY CHILDREN'S BOOKS, and the Diana logo
are trademarks of Bloomsbury Publishing Plc

First published in the United States of America in February 2023
by Bloomsbury Children's Books

Bloomsbury books may be purchased for business or promotional use. For information
on bulk purchases please contact Macmillan Corporate and Premium Sales Department at
specialmarkets@macmillan.com

Library of Congress Cataloging-in-Publication Data
Names: Schwartz, Ella, 1974- author. | Williams, Lily, illustrator.
Title: Is it okay to pee in the ocean? / by Ella Schwartz ; illustrated by Lily Williams.
Description: New York : Bloomsbury Children's Books, 2023. | Includes bibliographical references. | Audience: Ages 8-12 |
Audience: Grades 4-6
Summary: Explore the human systems that make pee happen, tackle environmental questions about the impacts of
human waste, discover surprising uses of urine throughout history—like in mouthwash and skin creams—and even
try out at-home, hands-on experiments (with no bodily fluids required, of course!) —Provided by publisher.
Identifiers: LCCN 2022029840 (print) | LCCN 2022029841 (e-book)
ISBN 978-1-68119-5131 (hardcover) • ISBN 978-1-5476-0145-5 (e-book)
Subjects: LCSH: Urine—Juvenile literature. | Urine—History—Juvenile literature. |
Urine—Environmental aspects—Juvenile literature.
Classification: LCC QP211 .S34 2023 (print) | LCC QP211 (e-book) | DDC 612.4/61—dc23/eng/20220720
LC record available at https://lccn.loc.gov/2022029840
LC e-book record available at https://lccn.loc.gov/2022029841

Book design by Yelena Safronova
Typeset by Westchester Publishing Services
Printed in China by C&C Offset Printing Co., Ltd., Shenzhen, Guangdong
2 4 6 8 10 9 7 5 3 1

To find out more about our authors and books visit www.bloomsbury.com
and sign up for our newsletters.

For Harrison, Sammy, and Nate, who have peed in the ocean and elsewhere

—E. S.

To Grandpa Joe, D.D.S. Thank you for always encouraging my love of science and making curiosity fun.

—L. W.

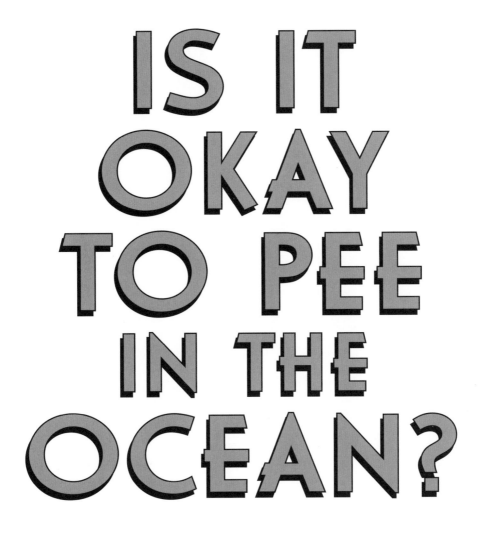

CONTENTS

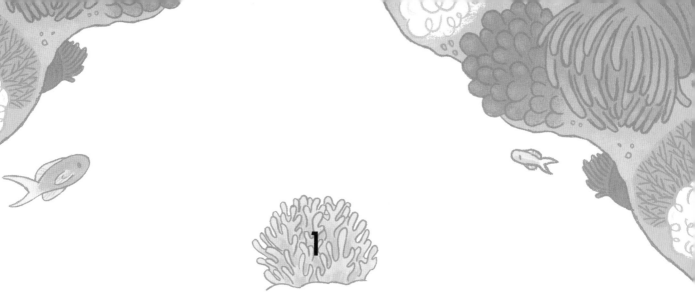

IS IT OKAY TO PEE IN THE OCEAN?

Don't say it's never happened to you.

You know it has.

You finally get to the beach, unpack the car, trudge through the hot sand, lay out your beach blanket, and realize . . . you gotta go.

"Mom! I have to go to the bathroom!"

Mom rolls her eyes. "Just go in the ocean," she says, reaching for a tube of sunscreen.

Pee in the ocean?

"But isn't there a real bathroom somewhere?"

She points a finger at the waves breaking against the shore. "Go. In there. Everybody does it."

Well, if everybody does it . . .

You march into the ocean, dodging the incoming waves until the water is just above your waist. By now, you really need to go. Okay, let's do this. But you're not sure how this is supposed to work. Do you just let it flow? Peeing in your bathing suit doesn't seem like such a good idea.

Just do it already! Even your mom said it was okay.

A quick check. Nobody is close enough to notice anything. Everybody in the water is otherwise occupied, splashing, jumping waves, or body surfing.

You'd better get on with it.

Here we go . . .

Don't worry about those kids playing over there. Look natural! They have no idea what you're doing. You're just hanging out in the ocean, cooling off. Ho-hum, ho-hum. They have no idea.

All finished?

Good.

You lunge backward because you don't want to be standing in a pool of your own pee for too long. Understandable. But you did it! You peed in the ocean. Feel better?

No?

You ask yourself, *did I just pollute the ocean?* Are those kids over there swimming in a pool of my pee? Is there some poor guppy or a great white shark out in the ocean choking on tainted water because of me? Did I just break the universe because I had to go to the bathroom?

Let's answer that question: No. You didn't break the universe. But it's an understandable concern. Is it really okay to pee in the ocean? Does peeing in the ocean affect the natural ecosystem? Does it harm sea life? Does it contaminate the waters so that beachgoers can no longer enjoy a fresh swim?

All good questions!

Let's find out.

2

WHY DO WE PEE?

Words Matter

Before figuring out if it's okay to pee in the ocean, you have to first understand what pee is. The technical term for pee is **urine**, and the technical term for peeing is **urinating**. But who says, *I need to urinate*? For some reason, many people are uncomfortable with the word *urinate*. Maybe it reminds them of going to the doctor. Maybe your doctor has asked you to urinate in a cup? Yeah, not fun.

The word *pee* was first used in the early eighteenth century. It is derived from the first letter of the word *pissier*, which means *to urinate* in Old French.

People call urine all sorts of things: "wee-wee," "tinkle," "pee-pee," and other expressions that are just too weird to list. But in this book, we agree to use the term *pee*, okay? Let's get used to the word. "Hey, I need to pee," or "Gross, it smells like pee in here!" Sound good?

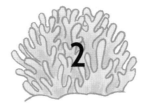

IF YOU CAME HERE LOOKING FOR A PEE JOKE . . . URINE LUCK!

PEEING ABROAD

It's stressful traveling to a foreign country and not being able to communicate in the local language. But imagine you're vacationing in some far-off land and you realize you need a bathroom. You ask a friendly-looking local, "Where's the bathroom?" and they respond with a look that screams, *what madness are you actually talking about?*

When it's time to go, there's no time for a language barrier, so before you get stuck with a desperate bathroom emergency, familiarize yourself with the local lingo.

In many European countries, like France, Germany, and the Netherlands, you're going to ask for the water closet, which sounds like it should come equipped with a dressing room and wardrobe, but really is nothing more than a traditional bathroom.

In Australia, if you ask for the bathroom you'll probably get sent to a room with a bath, which is often not in the same room as the toilet. Australians call the bathroom a *dunny*. Fun fact: in an Australian dunny, when you flush the toilet, the water swirls in the opposite direction as in America.

In the United Kingdom you pee in the *loo*, and in Japan you do your business in the *benjo*.

To be fair, even in America, public toilets are known by many different names, including *restrooms*, *comfort stations*, and *washrooms*.

Going to Waste

But what is peeing all about anyway? Everybody does it, but what exactly *is* it?

Here's the simple answer: Pee is waste. It's the stuff your body doesn't need. What do you do with the stuff in your house you don't need? You get rid of it! Your body does the same thing. It gets rid of the stuff it doesn't need, the waste. Your pee is liquid waste. There are other kinds of waste your body produces, like sweat and—you guessed it—poop. But we're not going to talk about that kind of waste in this book.

Another word for this waste is **by-product**. You can think of it this way—let's say you're making a painting. You need paint, right? But you don't need the container the paint comes in. That's a by-product you can throw away. You need water to dip your paintbrush in, but once you're done painting you can spil that murky water down the drain. That's another by-product. How does your body end up with all this waste it needs to get rid of? Body processes like **digestion** (breaking down the food you eat) and **metabolism** (turning the food you eat into energy) produce by-products. Just like the by-products that are created from painting, your body makes all kinds of by-products as it works to keep you going all day.

So how does that milkshake you had for breakfast end up in your toilet bowl, or, in this case, the ocean? Well, your pee doesn't actually contain milkshake, or juice, or hot chocolate. It does contain water, though. Pee is your body's main way of controlling the amount of water in your system. Have you ever noticed that when you drink a lot, you pee more? That's your body doing its job, controlling how much water it keeps and sending everything it doesn't need away.

But pee isn't just about getting rid of the water in the milkshake you had for breakfast. Water is a big part of your pee, but there are other by-products your body has to get rid of too—like urea, creatinine, and urochrome. We'll talk more about these fancy science words later. In the meantime, there's much more to learn about pee! Pee may be waste, but it's not unimportant.

DON'T TRY THIS AT HOME

American pioneers treated earaches by pouring warm pee in their ears and then plugging them with cloth. Some people today still think this is good medicine for an ear infection, but most doctors agree it's a bad idea and would never recommend this treatment.

ROMAN RITUALS

Yes, pee is your body's waste, but waste isn't always useless. In fact, pee was considered to be very valuable in ancient Rome. It was used to remove tough stains from clothes. Pee was considered so important that the streets of Rome were often lined with containers to collect pee from passersby. Once full, the contents would be taken to the laundry and poured over dirty clothes. A worker would then stand in a tub of urine and dirty clothes, stomping on the garments until the stubborn stains disappeared.

If you think the ancient Romans were pretty gross for washing their clothes in pee, what would you say if someone told you they also washed their mouth with pee? It's true! The ancient Romans believed that rinsing their mouth with pee gave them a whiter smile. While it may be true that their teeth looked shinier, it probably didn't do much to help their breath smell fresher.

IS IT OKAY TO PEE IN THE OCEAN?

3

HOW DO I PEE WHEN STANDING ON MY HEAD?

Pee leaves your body through the **urinary system**. The urinary system is the term for the body parts and the pathway that regulate body fluids and eliminate liquid waste. In other words: all the parts that deal with pee. The urinary system is sometimes called the **urinary tract** or **renal system**. You might think peeing is easy. You don't really need to think about peeing. You just do it! But a lot of internal body parts and organs must work together flawlessly to make pee happen.

The urinary system is in every person, big and small, and it does the same job no matter where they decide to let their pee loose. Whether your pee's final destination is a toilet bowl, a hole in the ground, or the ocean, everybody goes through the exact same process to make pee.

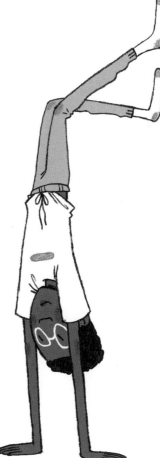

Filter Pump

The first stop on the urinary tract is your **kidneys**. The kidneys are so important that most people have two of them, even though we need only one to survive. Think of this as your body having a backup. Just in case something goes wrong with one kidney, you'll have a spare.

The kidneys are bean-shaped organs about the size of your fist. Every drop of blood in your body passes through your kidneys as many as four hundred times each day! Your kidneys are always working, even when you're sleeping. In a lifetime, the kidneys clean more than 1 million gallons of liquid. That's enough to fill a small lake!

WHEN KIDNEYS NEED SOME HELP

Since kidneys have the very important job of keeping the blood in your body clean, it's especially important to keep them strong and healthy. But sometimes people don't have healthy kidneys. If kidneys stop working well, a person may need help from science and medicine to make sure their blood stays clean. **Dialysis** is one common medical treatment for kidney problems. When a patient is on dialysis, a machine works in place of the kidneys to filter the blood. Instead of the patient's blood being cleaned by their kidneys, the blood travels through a machine which does the job of cleaning. Once the blood is cleaned, the dialysis machine returns the cleaned blood to the patient. The process doesn't hurt but can take a lot of time. Each dialysis session usually lasts a few hours, and most patients will need dialysis several times a week to make sure their blood stays healthy.

IS IT OKAY TO PEE IN THE OCEAN?

GIVER OF LIFE

When a person's kidneys are no longer healthy or operating properly, that person has **renal disease** or **kidney failure**. People who have renal disease typically require dialysis, but sometimes even dialysis is no longer effective. In that case, a kidney transplant may be an option. A kidney transplant is a special kind of surgery where the diseased kidney is replaced with a healthy kidney from a donor. Sometimes, a donor kidney comes from a person who has died but previously agreed to donate their kidney to help save someone's life. In other cases, the kidney may come from a living donor who is a good match and is able and willing to donate one of their kidneys.

Kidneys are the most commonly transplanted organ. More than 28,000 kidney transplants are performed every year, and the success rate of kidney transplants is very high. But this wasn't always the case. The first human kidney transplant was performed in 1933 by Soviet surgeon Yuri Voronov. The recipient was a 26-year-old woman who received a kidney from a deceased 60-year-old man. The recipient died two days later. In 1954 the first successful kidney transplant was performed by Joseph Murray in Boston, Massachusetts. During this procedure, a kidney was successfully transplanted between identical twins. For this accomplishment, Joseph Murray was awarded the prestigious Nobel Prize in medicine.

The kidneys' main job is to filter waste from your blood and produce pee. They do this with the help of more than a million tiny filters called **nephrons**. If the

HOW DO I PEE WHEN STANDING ON MY HEAD?   11

kidneys stopped working, **toxins** (bad stuff) would build up in your body and make you very sick. If the kidneys do a good job, they send pure, clean blood back to your heart. You don't want dirty blood going to your heart.

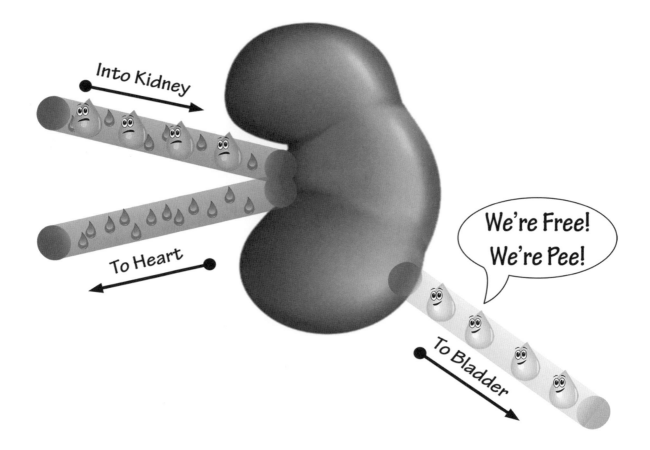

Your kidneys have produced pee. Great! Now what?

Sea IT FOR YOURSELF

What you'll need:

- Two clear jars or drinking glasses
- Water
- A scoop of sand or dirt
- Red food coloring (optional)
- Coffee filter
- Rubber band

Fill one jar with water. If using food coloring, place a few drops into the water. This liquid represents blood. Next, drop a scoop of sand or dirt into the "blood." The sand or dirt represents waste products floating in blood. Now, use the rubber band to affix the coffee filter over the mouth of the second, empty jar. This coffee filter will function like a kidney. Carefully pour the solution you've made through the coffee filter and into the second jar. Watch how the kidney (coffee filter) traps the waste (sand) and sends clean blood (liquid) into the bottom of the jar. Notice all the waste trapped in the coffee filter. In kidneys, this waste would be taken to the bladder in the form of urine to be removed from the body.

The Journey Continues

Your pee now continues on its path through your urinary tract. Next stop? The **ureters**. These are thin tubes that carry pee away from the kidneys. You have two ureters, one coming out of each kidney. The ureters point downward, and pee naturally wants to travel downward thanks to the force of gravity. But what happens if you're lying down or even standing on your head? Does the pee travel in the opposite direction through your ureters and back to your kidneys? No. Not even if you decide to stand on your head for a really long time. Don't bother trying this out. All you'd get is a headache. In addition to gravity, the ureters use a wave of contractions—like a pumping action—to make sure the pee travels away from the kidneys and not toward them. Once pee leaves the kidneys, there is no coming back! The ureters make sure of that.

The next stop on your pee's journey is your **bladder**. The bladder is a sac that holds the pee until you decide it's time to go to the bathroom. Think of the bladder as a waiting room for your pee. It is made of stretchy material that swells up like a balloon as it gets fuller. When your bladder is really full, you have to go really bad. Your bladder actually communicates with your brain to tell you when it might be time to find a bathroom. This message is transmitted by your bladder to your brain using tiny sensors called **nerves** that can detect when your bladder is starting to get a little too full.

Once this happens, your brain sends you a message that it's time to go. As soon as you give the signal, your pee travels from your bladder through a small passageway called the **urethra** and finally finds the light of the world outside your body.

Peeing might not seem like a big deal, but inside your body lots of parts work together to help you go. Remember, pee is waste, and luckily your body is smart enough to know how to eliminate the waste from your blood and shuttle it out of your body. Peeing is all part of keeping your body healthy!

SO SCARY!

Have you ever been so terrified you actually wet your pants? Even just a teeny tiny bit? It's okay! It turns out it wasn't your fault. You had absolutely no control over this. Blame your brain! Your brain is doing exactly what it's supposed to do when you are confronted with what it thinks might be a dangerous situation. It tries to protect itself. This is called a **fight or flight** reaction. It's the same reaction your brain may have if, for example, a scary-looking grizzly bear starts running toward you. What are you going to do? Your brain will compel you to run as fast as you possibly can. You don't think about it. You just do it. It's called instinct. This same fight or flight instinct is to blame when you wet your pants from fear. When you're really, really scared, your brain may produce signals that override your bladder control, so you pee—whether you want to or not.

And humans aren't alone in peeing when frightened. Pigeons will pee when chased. Laboratory animals, like mice and rats, have a reputation for peeing on researchers' hands while being handled. Gazelles in the savannah have been known to pee when being pursued by predators. So it's a natural reaction, even though it may be a whole lot embarrassing.

"I'M GOING TO EXPLODE!"

You've heard people say it.

"If I don't find a bathroom right now, my bladder is going to explode!"

But is it really possible for someone's bladder to explode if they hold their pee in for too long?

Nope. You don't have to worry about your bladder exploding into messy bits. A bladder won't actually burst.

However, doctors recommend when you need to go, you should just go. If someone holds their pee in too often, they may be putting themselves at risk of infection because too much bacteria could build up over time. Holding in your pee every so often isn't a big deal, but you shouldn't make it a regular habit.

IS IT OKAY TO PEE IN THE OCEAN?

ISN'T PEE JUST YELLOW WATER?

Isn't pee just yellow water? Well, sort of, but not really. You are correct that pee is *mostly* water. In fact, on average, 95 percent of your pee is water. The exact percentage will depend on how much fluid you've consumed, but in general, the biggest component of your pee is good old H_2O.

But pee isn't simply water!

Remember how the kidneys' main job is to clean blood destined for the heart? Well, all that "stuff" the kidneys remove is also part of pee.

What exactly is this stuff?

Sweaty Pee

Everyone's pee composition is different based on how their body works, the foods they've eaten, and environmental factors. But after water, the next biggest component of pee is **urea**. Urea is sometimes called carbamide. (Scientists sometimes like to give different names to the same thing. Maybe this makes scientists feel smarter, mostly because it makes everyone else confused.) Urea forms after your body breaks down proteins in foods you have eaten. Foods high in protein include meat, fish, yogurt, and beans. When your body breaks down (or, as fancy scientists might say, **metabolizes**) these important proteins, it produces urea as a by-product. Urea is also very important because any extra nitrogen your body needs to get rid of (another pesky by-product) is dissolved in urea. Nitrogen hitches a ride with urea and leaves your body through your pee.

By the way, peeing isn't the only way your body gets rid of urea. Urea is also released when you sweat. That's right, the sweat glistening across your skin on a hot day is kind of like pee.

WASTE NOT, WANT NOT

Inside the human body, urea is a waste that needs to be removed. But outside the human body, urea is actually very useful. For example, urea is sometimes added to skin creams and moisturizers, and it has been shown to be an effective treatment for many skin disorders, like eczema and psoriasis. No, this doesn't mean you're conditioning your skin with pee, but it does mean you're using a component *found* in pee. Slightly less gross, but effective!

Urea is also a popular fertilizer used by farmers to grow crops. It is often mixed into the soil, where its high nitrogen content is very beneficial for plant growth. Since human urine contains urea, scientists have experimented with using human pee to fertilize crops. After all, there is no shortage of human pee in the world, so we might as well put it to good use. Farmers have found that certain vegetables grew bigger and looked healthier in soil treated with pee than with more traditional fertilizers. Most important, the vegetables tasted delicious, with no pee taste detected!

Golden Yellow

Incidentally, urea is colorless and odorless, so if you thought that urea might be the reason your pee is yellow or smelly, you'd be mistaken. What makes your pee yellow is actually **urochrome**. The magic of urochrome begins in your liver, another very important organ in your body. One of the jobs your liver performs is to break down old, dead blood cells. Most of the by-product of this process gets sent through your intestine and out of your body through your poop. In fact, your poop derives its brownish color from this blood-cell by-product. But not all of it is destined for your poop. Some of this by-product is transported to your kidneys, where it gets filtered and converted to urochrome before exiting your body through your pee as a lovely shade of yellow.

ARE YOU PEEING BLING?

Alchemy is an ancient practice that sought to turn metal into gold. Some early alchemists believed that the yellow color of pee might be from actual gold. They performed all kinds of experiments trying to pull gold out of pee. They all failed miserably. But while experimenting with pee, one German alchemist, Henning Brand, did make an interesting discovery. He didn't find gold in pee, but he did discover phosphorus. His discovery must have been very exciting to an alchemist of his time because the phosphorus glowed a pale green color and never burned out. Brand must have thought this was pretty cool, even though it wasn't gold.

This picture, titled *The Alchemist in Search of the Philosopher's Stone*, was painted in 1771 and depicts Brand's discovery of phosphorus.

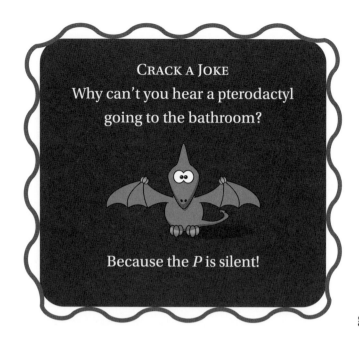
Of course, you've probably noticed that sometimes your pee is very bright yellow and sometimes it is clearer. This has to do with how much fluid you've taken in on a particular day. When your body has just the right amount of water, your pee is a normal buttercup color. On days when you drink too much water (yes, it's possible to drink too much water!), your pee is nearly clear because the urochrome is overly diluted. If your pee is a deep yellow, it could be a sign of dehydration, so grab yourself a glass of water!

PEE PREDICTOR

In ancient Egypt, women had some strange pee customs!

A woman would pee on wheat and barley seeds over the course of several days. If the barley grew, it supposedly meant the woman was pregnant with a boy baby. If the wheat grew, it allegedly meant the woman was pregnant with a girl baby. If neither of the seeds sprouted, it meant she was not pregnant at all.

It turns out, this pee pregnancy predictor wasn't all that farfetched. Modern testing of this pee prophecy in a lab found that 70 percent of the time the urine of pregnant women did, in fact, promote seed growth, while the urine of non-pregnant women and men did not. Scientists believe this has to do with certain elevated hormone levels in pregnant women's urine.

And what if your pee isn't yellow at all, but red, blue, or black? Then you've got a mystery to solve! A good bet is you probably ate something to make your pee a weird color. Have you eaten beets recently? You may have **beeturia**, a term used to describe peeing red or pink after eating a lot of beets. Don't worry. This is not serious! Your pee will return to its normal hue in no time. Other foods and even some medications may also turn your pee odd colors. But if you start peeing rainbow colors, you should seek medical attention immediately. That's just plain weird.

STINKY GREENS

Asparagus is super healthy for you, but if you've ever eaten asparagus, the next time you went to the bathroom you may have noticed your pee smelled a little weird.

In a letter penned by Benjamin Franklin in 1781, he wrote, "*A few stems of asparagus eaten, shall give our urine a disagreable odour* [*sic*]." And the same is true if you eat asparagus today!

So why does your pee smell funky after eating asparagus? It starts with a natural chemical found in asparagus called asparagusic acid. When your digestive system breaks down the asparagusic acid, a smelly sulfuric compound is produced as a by-product. When this compound is released in pee, most people detect a foul-smelling odor.

Some people, however, don't detect anything unusual. For them, this asparagus pee smells like their normal pee. Scientists believe this has to do with genetic factors. Even if you can't smell the pee, it doesn't mean your body isn't producing the compound and that other people can't smell your asparagus pee. And while asparagus pee smells are not harmful, be sure to flush the toilet to get rid of the odor.

More Ingredients

But that's not all! Your pee is filled with so much more that we haven't talked about yet!

Did you know that every time you use your muscles they produce waste? And where do you think that waste goes? Of course! Into your pee. Let's try it. Make a muscle. Come on, you can do better than that! A big muscle? That's all you've got? Okay, it'll do. You just used **creatine** to make that muscle. Creatine supplies the energy that lets you show off those big muscles of yours. Actually, every time you walk, run, or jump, you're using muscles, and to do that you use creatine as the energy source.

CAN YOU CRACK THE CODE?

Ancient Roman spies used pee as invisible ink to write secrets between the lines of their official documents. The messages would only appear when the pee ink was heated. If you didn't know to look for a hidden message, you'd have no reason to suspect a secret was hidden on the page. This is where the expression "read between the lines" comes from. It is also one of the earliest forms of **cryptography**, the science of keeping messages secret and hidden.

Creatinine is made from creatine. Yes, those words look very similar. Look very closely, though.

Creatinine and creatine.

Close, but not quite the same. You see the difference, right? Remember, scientists like to confuse us sometimes.

We shall not be fooled!

Where were we?

Oh right, creatinine. Creatinine is produced as the by-product when creatine (different word! Don't get confused!) is used for muscle movement. This by-product goes to—you guessed it!—the kidneys, where it gets filtered out of your blood and becomes part of your pee.

Bet you never thought your pee was this complicated, right? But we're not done yet! There are even more components that you'll find in pee. **Uric acid**, for example, is a by-product of food digestion. It's a good thing to pee out uric acid, because too much uric acid collecting in the body can cause joint inflammation, kidney stones, and other painful ailments.

And let's talk about salt. Not table salt, like the kind you put on your french fries or popcorn, but chemical salts, like sodium, chloride, and potassium. All of these are found in your pee. Although these *are* the same chemical salt elements that combine together to make table salt, it is not recommended that you taste pee to prove that it is, in fact, salty.

Pee Screening

To figure out what's really in your pee, doctors can perform a simple test. You may have gone to the doctor and been asked to pee in a cup. This is definitely not fun. It's pretty awkward, isn't it? The cups are usually teeny tiny, and you're always afraid you're going to miss and pee on your hand. And then once you've peed in the cup, what do you do with a cup full of pee? You need to walk around with it and hand it over to some stranger. It's so embarrassing! But you need to get over it, because a **urinalysis**, or urine test, is actually a very important part of making sure you're growing and staying healthy.

After you pee in the cup, your doctor will run tests on your pee to make sure your urinary system is working as it should. Some of these tests are performed right in your doctor's office. For other tests, your pee might be sent to a laboratory. Sometimes, when you're sick, your doctor might find something unusual in your pee. We're not talking about finding kryptonite or alien matter in your pee, although this could certainly indicate a problem. We're talking about finding bacteria or other germs in your pee, which could be a sign of kidney or bladder infection. In this case, the doctor would probably prescribe medicine to help get rid of the infection. So as annoying as it might be to pee in the cup, it is very important.

Leave your ego at the front desk and pee in the cup, okay?

STINKY KITTY

Think your cat may have peed somewhere in the house other than the litter box? Can you smell your cat's pee but you're not quite sure where exactly the odor may be coming from? Here's a clever trick: Grab a black light!

A cat's pee will glow under a black light because of its very high concentration of phosphorus. Human pee contains phosphorus too, but not in as high a concentration as cat pee. Human pee doesn't glow nearly as bright under a black light as cat pee.

You'll be a whiz at locating the source of feline fragrances.

5

WILL MY PEE HURT THE SEA?

You've been there before. You're having a great time at the beach, swimming in the ocean or jumping the waves, and . . . you need to go. There's probably a bathroom somewhere. But you need to get out of the water and trudge through the hot sand to get there. What's a beachgoer to do? Is it okay to pee in the ocean?

What happens when your pee mixes with the ocean water? Will it make the ocean dirty? Will it harm marine life? Is peeing in the ocean too gross to even think about?

Squeaky Clean

Some people think that if something is **sterile**, it is extra clean. But being clean isn't exactly being sterile. If you have clean socks, for example, it doesn't necessarily mean you have sterile socks. To explain this a bit, picture some socks that are *unclean* and *unsterile*. Admit it, you've had your fair

share of stinky, dirty socks. You probably have particularly nasty socks after running around sweating in your shoes. Luckily, you can wash the socks to freshen them up. They may no longer smell or have any dirt stains. You may think your socks are now clean, and you'd be right. They are clean. But they are not sterile. If you wanted sterile socks, you would need to make sure that the socks are not only clean, fresh, and stain-free, but also *germ*-free. You can't see germs, such as bacteria, but they're everywhere. Most of the germs all around us are not dangerous (and some are actually helpful), but to have a truly sterile object, it must be 100 percent free of germs. We don't *always* need, or want, to be in a completely sterile environment, but one example of an environment that is important to keep sterile is a surgery unit in a hospital, where patients could be at a high risk of getting sick from an infection. There, they would use strong cleaners to make sure no germs are present. People working in a surgical room typically wear gowns, gloves, and masks to prevent germs from spreading.

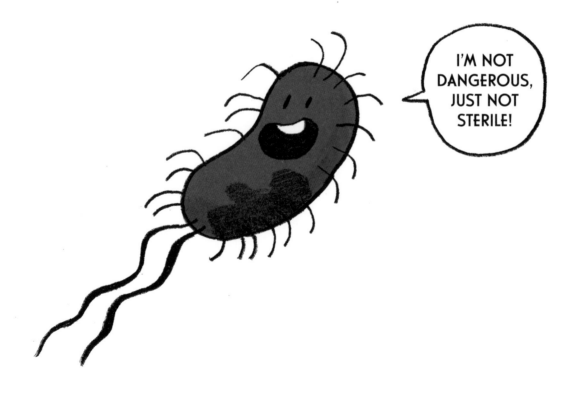

I'M NOT DANGEROUS, JUST NOT STERILE!

It turns out, pee from a healthy person is often considered sterile. That's right: Before pee exits a human, it is generally considered germ-free. In reality, studies show that in some cases pee may contain naturally occurring bacteria. These bacteria may be hanging out in your urinary system all the time. They don't make you sick, and they may actually help regulate your natural body chemistry. So even though a lot of scientists have held the belief for a long time that pee is sterile, that's not technically accurate because of these natural bacteria found in many people.

Why is mostly sterile pee so important, anyway? Well, you really don't have to worry about making the ocean unclean by peeing in it. There's nothing particularly dirty about pee. That doesn't mean you should drink it or anything like that! It may not be dirty, but it has elements that aren't safe to consume. Remember, your body worked hard to get rid of the by-products in your pee, so it's probably not a good idea to send it back into your system. But sending it into the ocean? Go for it!

CLEAN AND FRESH

If you are a healthy person, free of any infections, when your pee leaves your body it is considered sterile. But it doesn't stay sterile for very long. Once outside your body, pee can quickly attract bacteria. Bacteria love spending time in pee. It's the perfect environment for them to grow and multiply. In a short amount of time, bacteria can colonize a sample of pee. This is why, after some time, pee begins to smell. You're not smelling the pee; you're smelling the infestation of bacteria living on the pee. This is also one of the many reasons it's so important to wash your hands after using the bathroom. You don't want bacteria to find trace amounts of pee on your hands and decide to make that their new home.

Ingredients of the Sea

Still not convinced that pee is safe for the ocean? Since we've carefully studied the composition of pee, let's talk about how those components might affect the ecosystem. We already know that pee is mostly water. Guess what! The ocean is mostly water too. So introducing more water into the ocean isn't a problem.

What else is in ocean water? Most people who've swum in the ocean know the water tastes a little salty. That's because the ocean contains salt elements. About 3 percent of the ocean's mass comes from salt. If you've ever had ocean water splash into your eye, it may have stung for a few moments. That's from the salt. You may have also felt a little bit of a sting against your skin, especially if you had a small cut. That's also from the salt.

MYTH BUSTER

A sure way of ruining a nice day at the beach is getting stung by a jellyfish. A jellyfish's venom can cause a painful burning sensation. Usually a jellyfish sting isn't dangerous, but it's certainly unpleasant until the pain wears off.

There is a common myth that peeing on a jellyfish sting helps relieve the discomfort. Forget what you may have heard about this pee remedy! Not only is it gross, peeing on a jellyfish sting may actually make the symptoms worse. Don't pee on a jellyfish sting.

One of the most effective treatments for a jellyfish sting is applying vinegar to the area. So next time, try salad dressing instead of pee to nurse that pesky jellyfish sting.

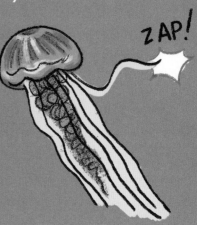

ZAP!

Sea IT FOR YOURSELF

Curious about how much salt is really in the ocean? Let's find out! What you'll need:

- About half a cup of ocean water—if you don't plan on visiting the beach anytime soon, you can simulate ocean water by mixing 1/2 cup of water with 1 teaspoon of salt
- Clean, clear-colored jar

Collect the ocean water in the jar and seal it closed until you get home. When you're ready to start the experiment, remove the jar lid and place the jar in a sunny, warm location, like a windowsill. Leave the jar undisturbed for several weeks. Observe the jar every few days and notice the water level decreasing. This process is called **evaporation**. As the water evaporates into the atmosphere, it leaves the salt behind. Once all the water has evaporated, notice how much salt remains in the jar. What does this tell you about the percentage of salt in ocean water?

SALTY SITUATION

Everybody who's ever swum in the ocean knows ocean water is salty. But if you think ocean water is salty, it's nothing compared to water in the Dead Sea, which is almost ten times saltier than ocean water. It is so salty that no plants, fish, or any other creatures are capable of living in it. That's why it's called the Dead Sea.

The Dead Sea is located between Israel and Jordan. Its unique desert location is what makes the water so salty. Water flows into the Dead Sea from the Jordan River, but then it has no way to escape. The region rarely gets any rain, so the salt content is never diluted. But soaring hot desert temperatures cause large quantities of water to evaporate, leaving a higher concentration of salt behind.

The Dead Sea is a very popular tourist destination. Due to the high salt content, beachgoers are able to float, effortlessly. The water is calm and warm, so it feels like floating in a pool with an invisible floatie under you. When swimmers come out of the water, their skin feels a bit oily, and as they dry off, layers of salt deposits remain. These salts are believed to have medicinal properties, easing skin problems and other medical conditions.

However, Dead Sea visitors are often warned not to pee in the Dead Sea, as this might cause a burning sensation. This theory has not been proven scientifically.

But wait! Your pee also contains salt elements—sodium, chloride, and potassium. Those components are the same as what's already in the salty ocean water. They've been there all along. In fact, there is a much higher concentration of these elements in the ocean than in your pee. Your pee salts are really not a concern in the big blue sea.

Still not confident peeing in the ocean is such a good idea? We need to talk about urea. Urea is one of the biggest components of human urine. Recall, urea is made as a by-product from breaking down proteins we eat in our diet. Urea also helps get rid of excess nitrogen in our body. But is urea harmful to the ocean?

The total volume of the Atlantic Ocean is 350 quintillion liters. That's 350 followed by eighteen zeroes. For the record, that's a crazy big number. The Atlantic Ocean is massive. Let's pretend for a minute that one day, every single person on the planet decides to pee in the Atlantic Ocean. What a crazy day that would be! If that day ever comes, then the ratio of pee to the ocean would be 60 parts per trillion.

That's pretty much nothing. It's less than a single grain of rice on a football field. Practically irrelevant. Remember that your pee is, quite literally, only a drop in the ocean.

Remember also that nitrogen is dissolved in urea. That nitrogen, when it enters the ocean, is converted into another element, called ammonia. Do you know what needs ammonia to grow and thrive? Ocean plant life. It turns out that the nitrogen-containing urea may actually be helpful for plants that make the ocean their home.

So if you thought you'd be breaking the universe by peeing in the ocean, you'd be mistaken. Nothing to worry about. It *is* okay to pee in the ocean.

6

IS THE OCEAN REALLY A TOILET?

You're still worried that peeing in the ocean could be harmful? What makes you think your pee is that special? You can't possibly think you're alone depositing your waste in the ocean. News flash! There are over 700,000 different species of animals that live in the oceans, and every one of them pees. That's a lot of pee! You think they're using a restroom and cleaning up after themselves? Of course not. Next time you go to the beach, try not to think about the fact that you're swimming in a big toilet bowl, okay?

FACE SPRAY

All sea animals pee. But some pee in pretty strange ways. Lobsters expel pee out of their faces. The lobster has a pair of pee blasters under its eyes. These blasters are connected to a supply of urine ammunition stored in two bladders, also located within a lobster's head. When a lobster is threatened, it shoots a steady stream of urine out of its face toward its target. To increase its peeing range, the lobster creates currents with its gills and mouth, further propelling the pee toward its target. A lobster's pee jet can reach a target five feet away!

So sometimes pee isn't just waste. It can be a weapon.

Impressive Peeing

One of the largest mammals in the world is the fin whale. Like many other large whale species, the fin whale population was severely impacted by whale hunting in the 1900s. As a result, the fin whale was placed on the endangered species list. But with the help of conservation policies and restrictions on whale hunting in the last several decades, the fin whale population has somewhat recovered. While the fin whale is still considered an endangered species, it is estimated that there are approximately 100,000 fin whales in the ocean today.

Fin whales can weigh over 80 tons and measure up to 80 feet long. They are heavier than ten average-sized elephants put together. A creature that big makes a lot of pee. How much pee? About 257 gallons per day. That's enough pee to fill more than three bathtubs! If you think one fin whale makes a lot of pee, imagine what the entire species of fin whales might do to the ocean. To better understand this, we need a little math.

IS IT OKAY TO PEE IN THE OCEAN?

If we take our estimated 100,000 fin whales and assume that each of those fin whales produces 257 gallons of pee per day, together all the fin whales in the world will produce:

100,000 x 257 = 25,700,000 gallons of pee per day.

That's more than 25 million gallons of pee a day! Another way to think about this? Well, an Olympic-sized swimming pool (which is a pretty big pool) contains more than 660,000 gallons of water.

Here's where we need more math.

If all the fin whales in the world produce more than 25 million gallons of pee per day, then that would fit into this many pools:

25,700,000 / 660,000 = 38.94

Rounding, we see that all the fin whales in the world would produce about 39 Olympic-sized pools' worth of pee.

Whoa.

That sounds like a whole lot of pee.

Except, in terms of the entire ocean, it really isn't. There is a lot of ocean on this planet, enough to fill 500 *trillion* Olympic-sized pools. So even with all those fin whales using the ocean as their bathroom, their pee accounts for a teeny tiny percent of the ocean's total water.

Even if whale pee built up every day for generations and generations, it still would be a small percentage of the total volume of the ocean.

BE THE CHANGE

Whales—and their pee—are critical to maintaining the ocean's delicate natural balance, so it's important to preserve the whale population. Whales may not be hunted by humans anymore, but human activity remains one of the biggest threats to whales' survival. Collisions with boats, becoming tangled in fishing nets, ocean pollution, and increased ocean noise all have a negative impact on the whales.

We can all do our part to protect the whale population. One of the most effective ways to help whales is to clean up garbage that could otherwise end up in the ocean. If you live near a beach, consider gathering some friends and family for a beach cleanup. Grab some gloves and trash bags and collect any garbage scraps you may find across the beach. Every scrap of trash you pick up is one less piece of trash that gets washed out to sea.

Another strategy to help whales is to sign petitions or write letters to elected officials asking them to increase whale protections.

IS IT OKAY TO PEE IN THE OCEAN?

Liquid Gold

But whale pee doesn't just sit around. As it turns out, whale pee is much more than waste. Whale pee feeds the ocean and safeguards the delicate balance of the ecosystem.

Whales generally find their food where the ocean is deep. They may dine at great depths. But when it's time for them to pee, they rise closer to the surface. After all, whales don't want to pee where they eat. Can you really blame them? Once they are ready to go, they rise up and release a massive stream of pee. Whale pee is full of nutrients that help ocean life thrive. In a way, whales act like a conveyor belt, moving nutrients from the food they eat, only available at great depths, up to the surface when they pee. Whale pee works almost like a fertilizer.

Phytoplankton, an important plant that mostly lives near the upper part of the ocean, is the foundation of all life in the ocean. It uses the nutrients in whale pee to grow. Without whale pee, phytoplankton could not survive. Without phytoplankton, other marine species, including whales, could not survive. Together, they keep the ocean ecosystem growing and thriving. And this is critically important to our planet.

THE AIR WE BREATHE

Phytoplankton and other marine plants produce more than 50 percent of the oxygen on Earth. In fact, phytoplankton have been making oxygen for more than 1 billion years longer than any plant found on land. Every breath of oxygen we take on land connects us to the ocean. That's one of the reasons keeping our oceans safe is so important.

Good Things Come in Small Packages

Of course, you might think that the pee from massive fin whales, great white sharks, giant manta rays, and other large sea creatures has the biggest impact on the ocean's ecosystem. And you wouldn't be wrong. These large sea creatures have the ability to spread their waste over thousands of miles, moving nutrients across wide spans where the ocean needs it most.

But what about all the little fish? They pee too! Doesn't their pee matter? Of course it does! Their tiny bodies may not produce the volume of pee of larger sea animals, but they are not pee slackers, either. Their pee makes a huge difference, especially for coral reefs and other coastal ecosystems where nutrients aren't abundantly available. That's because bigger fish, like whales and sharks, don't generally visit coral reef areas. So coral reefs depend on those little fish to sustain a nutrient balance.

CORAL CLUSTERS

Corals may look like rocks or plants, but they're actually animals. Coral is made up of individual organisms called **polyps**. Each polyp has a mouth surrounded by tentacles that sweep food and nutrients into its stomach. Waste is released from the same mouth opening. In other words, polyps pee out of their mouths.

Polyps live in groups of hundreds and sometimes thousands, which together form a coral colony. Coral polyps are usually clear, but they get their beautiful bright colors from different types of plants that grow together with the polyps.

The world's largest coral colony is the Great Barrier Reef in Australia. The Great Barrier Reef is so large it can be seen from outer space.

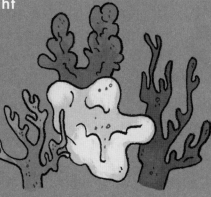

There are hundreds, sometimes thousands, of smaller fish species that hang out on reefs, so the corals are bathed in a steady flow of pee. The corals immediately gobble up the pee and use it for growth. And while the corals rely on the fish to provide them with nutrients to sustain their growth, the fish *also* rely on the coral reef for shelter and protection. This is called **symbiosis** or a **symbiotic relationship**. Symbiosis happens when two different creatures live together and help each other out. Neither can survive without the other. The fish need the coral reef for shelter and safety. The coral needs the fish for their pee. Everybody wins!

In case it wasn't obvious, pee is an ocean treasure.

BE THE CHANGE

The world's coral reefs are threatened and slowly being destroyed. Pollution and increasing ocean temperatures are a few of the reasons for the shrinking reefs. Some of the damage is even caused by human tourists. Visitors can damage the reefs by standing on them, touching them, or bumping into them with their boats. It's important to protect and preserve the reefs because so many animals call them home. The reefs are an important part of the ocean's ecosystem.

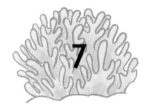

7

SO IS IT OKAY TO PEE ANYWHERE?

By now, you're probably convinced it's okay to pee in the ocean. Your pee is a mere drop in the bucket in our big blue sea. And it's not at all harmful to marine life. The next time you're at the beach and get the urge, avoid eye contact with other swimmers (because, let's face it, you don't need an audience to do your business) and feel free to pee in the ocean. It's perfectly safe and sensible.

But just because it's okay to pee in the ocean, you mustn't think it's okay to pee all over the place. If you have the option, it's always best to use a toilet. Don't forget to flush when you're all done. It's disturbing walking up to a toilet bowl and seeing it pre-filled with yellowy stuff. Pee that's left around breeds bacteria. That's why bathrooms sometimes have that gross smell. What you're getting a whiff of is bacteria that thrive in pee. So it's a good idea to flush that pee away. And—most important—always wash your hands when you're done to stop the spread of bacteria.

Most places where you shouldn't pee are obvious. You wouldn't pee in your living room, right? Peeing at the playground? Nope, that's just gross. But some places where you shouldn't pee might surprise you.

We Don't Swim in Your Toilet, So Don't Pee in Our Pool!

It might be tempting to pee in the pool. You're probably having so much fun swimming and playing. It might be chilly getting out of the pool, and your towel is way over there. It would be so much easier to just pee in the pool and not interrupt the fun.

But don't do that.

Peeing in the pool is *not* harmless.

Thanks to everything you've read in this book so far, you know peeing in the ocean is okay. You're an expert on peeing in the ocean! The ocean has ways of handling the pee. But that's not the case with pools.

The big difference between ocean water and pool water is that pool water is, essentially, motionless. You might say the pool water moves when swimmers swim, splash, or cannonball into it, and that's true. The water moves around a bit. But pool water doesn't move the way ocean water moves. Ocean water has currents and waves which keep the water in constant motion. Some currents can travel up to 75 miles in a single day! On the other hand, pool water is, for the most part, considered **stagnant**—which means it doesn't really go anywhere.

STOP THE ITCHY

Stagnant water can be found anywhere. A lagoon, puddles that form after a rainstorm, water that pools in a container—these are all examples of stagnant water sources, and all of them can be harmful if left undisturbed. In just a few days, germs may begin to form in these water sources. Sometimes stagnant water can become a breeding ground for animals that thrive in this environment, like mosquitoes. If you happen to find yourself the victim of too many mosquito bites while playing in the yard, you may want to look around for any nearby stagnant water sources. Eliminating these pools of water, even if they seem really small, could make a big difference.

Stagnant water has a tendency to attract germs. Some of these germs can make humans very sick, so pool operators work hard to keep them from growing in their pools. In addition to filtering systems, most pools use a chemical called chlorine to keep the germs at bay. Chlorine works like a disinfectant, eliminating infection-causing germs that get into pool water, and that's a very good thing.

Chlorine is great at attacking harmful germs in the pool water, but not so great at interacting with body fluids, including pee. It turns out that when chlorine interacts with pee, it produces a very strong chemical. If you've ever been to a pool, you know that it has a very distinct smell, and you've probably been told that's the smell of chlorine.

That's actually false.

That pool smell is chlorine combining with organic matter, which includes—you guessed it—human pee. In addition to pee, that chemical smell is produced when chlorine combines with human sweat. Who doesn't love jumping into a refreshing pool to cool off when they're super sweaty on a hot day? Well, when you do that, you're contributing to a chemical reaction.

IS IT OKAY TO PEE IN THE OCEAN?

The culprit is uric acid, which is of course found in pee, but also found in sweat. The uric acid combines with chlorine to produce a chemical called **chloramine**. The chlorine can also combine with other things on your body like dirt, oils, sunscreen, and even dead skin cells to produce other harmful by-products. Swimming pools tend to have lots of people floating and swimming around in the same water together, and those people have lots of things on their bodies that react with chlorine to produce chloramine. And that's why you smell that distinct pool odor. The smell is *actually* a chemical reaction between chlorine and all of the stuff humans drag into the pool. In fact, if there is an overpoweringly strong chemical smell at the pool, it probably means a lot of the chlorine is combining with human pee, poop, sweat, and other gross stuff instead of working to destroy bacteria in the pool. A strong chemical smell usually means it's time to add more chlorine. You might

HOW GROSS IS THAT POOL?

Usually, the swimming pool is a super fun and safe way to enjoy a hot summer day. But occasionally, if a pool isn't well maintained, it may not be the best idea to dive right in. There are some good clues to look for to help determine if the pool is clean and safe.

Take a look at the water. Can you see straight to the bottom of the pool? Cloudy water could mean an overgrowth of germs. You should avoid the pool if it looks murky.

Next, feel the pool wall. Does it feel icky or slimy? If it does, that may mean there are germs living in the pool. It's probably best not to go in.

And last, take a good whiff. All pools have a slight chemical smell, but be wary if there is a very strong smell. This could be a sign of chlorine reacting with unwanted by-products.

Otherwise, you're good to go!

SO IS IT OKAY TO PEE ANYWHERE?

think you're smelling chlorine at the pool, but you're really smelling chloramine. Indoor pools usually have a stronger chloramine smell because the area isn't well ventilated, like outdoor pools.

Chloramine can be very dangerous when inhaled in large quantities. It could make it hard to breathe, produce itchy red eyes, and even irritate your skin. In very large quantities it might cause asthma and damage internal organs. But, before you proclaim that you're never going to the pool again, don't worry! A small amount of chloramine isn't going to make you sick. Even if a lot of people peed in the pool, it would be pretty gross, but mostly harmless. There isn't enough chloramine in the pool to justify staying away from swimming entirely.

The truth is, it's nearly impossible to eliminate all dirt, sweat, lotions, makeup, deodorant, and, yes, pee, in a swimming pool. Inevitably, these components will combine with chlorine in the pool to produce that strong pool smell. So why use chlorine at all? Because without chlorine there would be a large buildup of bacteria, like *E. coli* and salmonella, which are far more dangerous to humans than a little chloramine. By comparison, chloramine is just a nuisance.

Yet, there are steps you can take to make it safer, and cleaner, to swim in the pool. The most obvious, of course, is to never ever pee in the pool. It might be annoying to halt the fun to look for a bathroom, but this is the easiest way swimmers can help keep the pool clean. Ironically, the dirtiest pools tend to be the ones where professional swimmers work out for long hours at a time. These swimmers are discouraged, oftentimes by their coaches, from interrupting their demanding workouts for a bathroom break. They have no choice but to pee in the pool. Olympic swimmers Michael Phelps and Ryan Lochte have both admitted to routinely peeing in the pool. Bad idea. Just don't do it.

Another important step you can take to keep the pool clean is to shower before entering the pool. A quick rinse will wash away any sweat or dirt you may have on your body.

Big Fish in a Small Pond

Just like at the swimming pool, it's usually not okay to pee in small bodies of water like ponds and lakes. A little pee in a lake, from the frogs, fish, and other creatures that live there, is fine. But a whole lot of extra pee from humans could be very destructive.

When swimmers pee in a lake, pond, or other smaller body of water, they introduce elements from their pee that don't naturally occur in these environments in such high concentrations, like phosphorus and nitrogen, for example. These elements can promote the growth of algae. A little algae growth is fine. Algae naturally live in these waters and actually are a good source of food and nutrients for some of the creatures they share their environment with. But when algae grow too much or too quickly, this is called an **algal bloom**.

Algal blooms can be a big problem. When a lot of algae suddenly burst across the surface of the water, they can block the sunlight from other freshwater plants growing at the bottom of the water. This can cause those plants to die off. An algal bloom can also attract a whole lot of extra bacteria in the water, especially when the algae themselves start to die off. This happens because when algae die, bacteria that decompose the dead plants use up the oxygen in the water. With less oxygen in the water, the fish that need that oxygen may suffocate and die.

Algal blooms can happen in small lakes or vast oceans, but they can grow out of control much more quickly in smaller bodies of water. When this happens, the lake or pond can get very smelly and look frothy and foamy. It's usually not a good idea to swim in algal bloom–infested waters.

Not only is it a bad idea to pee *in* lakes and small bodies of water, it's also a bad idea to pee *near* them. The reason is that when waste is nearby, after a heavy rainfall the rainwater will carry that waste straight into the lake. This is true not only for human waste, but also for other contaminants that may have been deposited near the body of water. Heavy rain will pick up anything it meets as it drains into nearby waters.

Forecast: Risk of Showers

And what about peeing in the shower? You might think that the whole point of taking a shower is to come out cleaner than when you went in. You don't want to end up dirtier, and nobody wants a filthy shower stall.

But the truth is, it's probably okay to pee in the shower. And in some ways, peeing in the shower rather than a toilet bowl is actually good for the environment, and here's why. Even though it may seem like our planet has a ton of water in our oceans, that water is salty. Fresh water is an important and dwindling resource. We need fresh water to drink, bathe, and farm, and this fresh water is very precious. Scientists are concerned that humans are consuming fresh water too quickly. This overuse, especially when combined with climate change, could lead to a future of water shortages and droughts. Already, in some parts of the world, billions of people lack access to clean fresh water. We should be using our fresh water sensibly.

Flushing a toilet uses a lot of fresh water. Each flush uses several gallons of water, and since the average American flushes a toilet five times a day, the amount of fresh water used to carry your pee and poop away can really add up!

When you pee in the shower, you're skipping a flush. The water is already running, ready to carry your pee down the drain. In some ways, your shower is doing double duty: getting you clean while saving water by eliminating a flush.

But, you might be saying, peeing on yourself won't help you get clean in the shower. It'll just make the shower dirty. Think about what you're doing in the shower, though. You're using the shower to wash away all the yucky stuff that has accumulated on you throughout the day. This includes dirt, mud, sweat, and who knows what else you may have picked up on your skin or in your hair as you've gone about your day. You've likely washed off other gross things from your body, sending them down the drain. Should you really worry about pee? And if you happen to get a little pee on yourself, you're in the right place. Just grab that soap and wash yourself.

But while it may be okay to pee in *your own* shower, it's a different story when it comes to public showers. This is because most people's pee is safe, but sometimes, when people have an infection, their pee contains bacteria, and there's a risk it could remain on the shower floor. For that matter, you never really know what could be hiding in public showers. Public showers may not have the best cleaning standards, especially in high-traffic areas like public beaches. Not only could they have remnants of bacteria from pee and other sources, but they could have mold and other contaminants.

For this reason, it's common courtesy not to pee in a public shower. And for your own health, if you are showering in a public shower, make sure you wear shower shoes, especially if you have cuts or scratches on the bottoms of your feet. You don't want to risk having invisible germs touch your skin and possibly cause an unwanted infection.

So, in case you're keeping score . . .

Peeing in the ocean? Safe. Go for it.

Peeing in the pool? Nope.

Peeing in or near the pond? Negative.

Peeing in the shower? For the most part okay, but be smart about it.

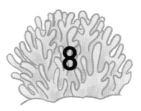

WHAT'S SO SPECIAL ABOUT THE SEA?

We've already established that peeing in the ocean isn't harmful, but why does it matter anyway? Why worry about protecting our planet's oceans when we live on land and not at sea? Well, we might be land dwellers, but Earth is mostly a water planet. Oceans cover about 70 percent of Earth. That's why Earth appears blue when viewed from outer space. Without the oceans, we wouldn't have much of a planet. Earth's oceans are vitally important not just to fish and sea creatures but to every living thing on this, your planet Earth.

Carbon Dioxide Away

When you breathe, you're taking in oxygen and releasing carbon dioxide. Without oxygen, you couldn't breathe, which means you couldn't live. Where do you think the oxygen we breathe comes from? Some of that oxygen comes from trees and plants on land, especially forests, but most oxygen actually comes from the oceans. The ocean produces oxygen through plants that live there, like phytoplankton, sea kelp, and algae. The oxygen is released by these plants as a result of **photosynthesis**. Photosynthesis is a process by which plants convert carbon dioxide from the atmosphere into the energy they need to grow and thrive. Oxygen is released as a by-product of photosynthesis, and while oxygen may be a waste product to ocean plants, it is vitally important to land animals. You can thank the ocean for at least half of the oxygen you breathe in every day.

LIGHT
CARBONDIOXIDE

OXYGEN

The ocean also plays a starring role in cleaning up the messes humans make when we burn fossil fuels, drive cars, and run big factories. These activities are all sources of air pollution, generating a lot of carbon dioxide. While it's true that carbon dioxide is created naturally every time we exhale, industrial activity produces excessive amounts of carbon dioxide. These emissions contribute to climate change and global warming. We're lucky the ocean is so great at sucking up carbon dioxide from the air. While the oceans can't fix the carbon dioxide problem on their own, without the oceans Earth would be in even bigger trouble.

ONE GLOBAL OCEAN

Traditionally, we think of planet Earth as having five oceans: the Atlantic, Pacific, Indian, Arctic, and Southern oceans. In actuality, the five oceans are all connected together, so it's really one big ocean broken up by different land masses. The ocean is so vast that only a very small fraction has been explored. In fact, the ocean is less explored than the surface of Mars!

Always on the Move

Not only do we have oceans to thank for combatting global warming, but oceans also get credit for regulating temperatures across the map. If you've ever been to a beach (whether or not you peed in the ocean), you know the ocean water is constantly moving. Ocean water can move for several reasons.

The first reason is the gravitational pull from the sun and the moon, which causes **tides**. As the Earth rotates, the moon and the sun's gravity pull on the ocean water. This creates periods of high tide, when the water level rises, and low tide, when the water level falls, each day.

Ocean movement is also affected by wind. As wind blows over the water, it pushes against the water's surface, producing waves. You've probably seen waves caused by winds crashing against the shore.

Ocean currents are another way the ocean moves. Currents form across the ocean because of changes in water's **salinity,** the amount of salt dissolved in the water. The higher the salinity of the water, the denser (or heavier) it becomes. The denser, saltier water sinks, which creates a current of movement.

Currents can also form because of differences in the ocean's temperature. Cold water is denser than warm water, and the denser, colder water sinks, creating movement and currents.

Currents can move a lot of water great distances. Currents also keep ocean water from getting too cold or too hot. The hottest place on Earth tends to be near the equator, while the coldest places on Earth are near the south pole and north pole. By moving warmer water from the equator to the poles via currents, oceans prevent the poles from getting too cold. Likewise, by moving the icy water from the poles toward the equator, the oceans keep the beaches near the center line of our planet from overheating.

But this doesn't affect only the temperature of the water itself. It also impacts the surrounding air temperature. Think about the feeling you experience when your hands hover over a steaming mug of hot chocolate. Your hands feel warm and toasty. This is the same thing that happens with the oceans but on a much bigger scale. When ocean temperatures are warm, they warm the surrounding air, leading to a rise in air temperatures. And since oceans cover most of the Earth's surface, they have a lot of control over our planet's climates.

It Comes from the Sea

But that's not all we should thank the ocean for! Fish and shellfish that come from the ocean are a primary source of animal protein for more than 3 billion people—that's nearly half the world's population! Without the ocean, humans would be missing out on one of our most vital food sources. The ocean is home to countless fish and shellfish that people enjoy eating. Some of the most popular seafood options are cod, shrimp, salmon, tuna, lobster, and crab. Sushi, a dish consisting of raw fish, originated in Japan but is now consumed worldwide. Fish and chips is a popular food from the United Kingdom. In Spain, you can enjoy the national dish called *paella de marisco*, made from rice and various kinds of shellfish, like mussels, shrimp, and crab. A full menu comes from the sea!

And let's talk about seaweed, which is actually a terrible name for something very important. Most "weeds" are annoying, unwanted plants that grow uncontrollably and might spoil a beautiful lawn, but that's not what seaweed is at all. Seaweed is just a common name for all different kinds of water plants and algae that grow in the ocean, as well as rivers, lakes, and other bodies of water. Seaweed provides food and shelter for marine organisms but also serves as food for people. Have you ever tried eating seaweed? You may have had some without even knowing it! Ingredients made from seaweed can be found in all kinds of food, like ice cream, chocolate milk, and yogurt. You'll even find seaweed in some toothpaste and skincare products. Seaweed is also used in medicines.

Sea IT FOR YOURSELF

What you'll need:

- Glass or clear-colored baking pan
- Cold water
- About 12 ice cubes
- 2 cups of boiled water
- Red and blue food coloring
- Plastic fish or sea-creature toys (optional)

Fill the container about halfway with cold water. Mix in 2–3 drops of blue food coloring and ice cubes. Wait a few minutes so the water gets cold. You want the water to be as cold as possible. If you're using toy fish, place them inside your ocean now for added fun! Then, place 2–3 drops of red food coloring into the boiled water. Carefully and slowly pour the red, hot water onto one side of your blue ocean.

What's going on here? You've simulated an ocean current! Deep water currents are formed as a result of differing water temperatures. The wide difference in temperature causes the water to move great distances. Eventually the water mixes together to create lukewarm water, which is how it works in the ocean (although the ocean doesn't turn purple!).

Beyond the necessities oceans give us, they also offer loads of recreational activities. Swimming, sailing, surfboarding, water skiing, and fishing are just a few examples of fun people can enjoy at the ocean. The ocean is also beautiful and calming just to watch. It can be a source of relaxation and can inspire poetry, art, and music. Can you think of any books or art inspired by the sea?

So, even if you've never been to the ocean, the ocean has come to you. With every breath you take, you have the ocean to thank. Maybe you've enjoyed a fish dinner. Even if you're not a fish lover, you've probably eaten treats that were derived from the ocean. Perhaps you've read a poem inspired by the majesty of the seas? The ocean is a part of all our lives.

TALES OF TAILS

Countless stories and mythologies have been inspired by the depths of the seas.

In Greek mythology, Poseidon was the god of the seas and was widely regarded as one of the most powerful gods of Olympus. He wielded a three-pronged spear called a trident and lived in an underwater palace. In ancient Greece, sailors would often pray to Poseidon for smooth sailing and safe passage. Today, you can visit an ancient temple of Poseidon near Athens, Greece.

The kraken is a giant squid-like sea monster from Norse mythology that attacked sailors. There is no scientific proof that krakens ever haunted the ocean, but deep-sea giant squids are real. The longest squids recorded measured more than 40 feet! That's longer than a city bus!

Stories of mermaids, magical half-human, half-fish beings, have long inspired storytellers. One of the earliest mermaid legends comes from ancient Assyria and dates back three thousand years. As the story goes, the goddess Atargatis accidentally caused the death of her daughter. In her grief and guilt, she dove into the water to end her life. But instead of death, she was transformed into what we now commonly refer to as a mermaid. Since then, countless mermaid stories have been told. Hans Christian Anderson's famous Danish fairy tale "The Little Mermaid" tells the story of a mermaid willing to give up her sea life for a human body. There are stories of mermaid-like creatures called sirens in Greek mythology who lure sailors to ruin on rocky coasts with their hypnotic songs. And while mermaids are not real, Christopher Columbus wrote in his journal about encountering mermaids during his historic voyage to the New World. Most people believe what he was really seeing was not a mermaid, but probably a manatee.

IF PEE DOESN'T POLLUTE THE OCEAN, WHAT DOES?

We know the ocean is enormous, way too big to be affected by our pee. But lots of other human activities *do* have a big effect on the ocean. The ocean is changing, primarily because of things we do. And massive changes, over a period of time, can hurt the ocean. When the ocean changes too drastically, there is a devastating effect not only on the plants and animals that call it home, but also on life on land. That's why it's important to understand the impact humans have on the ocean and how to minimize the strain we put on the seas.

Acids, Bases . . .

The ocean, of course, is made up of water. You may have heard water referred to as H_2O. The H stands for hydrogen and the O stands for oxygen. Each molecule of water contains two hydrogen atoms—hence that little 2 below the H—and one oxygen atom. The H_2O in the ocean has the same composition as the H_2O from a rainstorm, a river, or your bathtub. Water is water, when it comes to its chemical composition, but not all water is the same. This is because other elements might be mixed in with the molecules of H_2O. For example, ocean water has salt dissolved in it, which is, of course, not the case with the water that comes out of your faucet.

Ocean water also contains many minerals and nutrients that make it the perfect ecosystem for marine life. If any of these unique properties of ocean water changes, it could have a negative impact on everything that lives in the ocean. For example, at the poles of the earth, the frozen ice caps are melting and diluting the saltiness of the nearby water. Plants and animals living in these waters must either adapt to these changes or die.

Another important property of ocean water is its **acidity**. Acidity is a measurement of how much acid a substance contains. The opposite of an acid is a **base**, and the opposite of acidic is **basic**. The acidity of a substance is measured using what's called the **pH scale**, which runs from zero to 14. If something is neither acidic or basic, it is said to be neutral and has a pH number of 7. If something is acidic, it will have a pH number below 7. An example of an acidic substance is lemon juice. Have you ever sucked on a lemon? The super-tart, sour taste comes from acid. Lemon juice has a pH of about 2. Things that are basic have a pH greater than 7. Examples of basic substances include baking soda and cleaning agents.

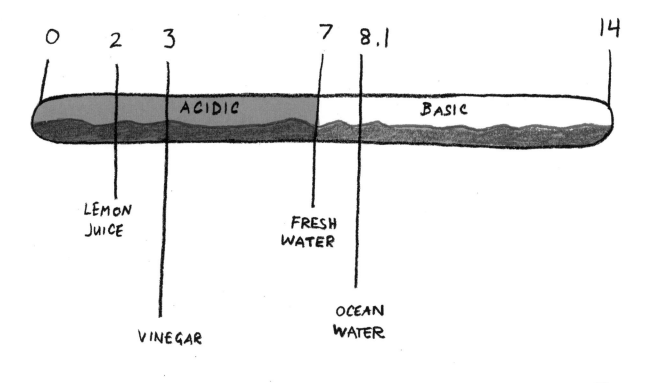

Drinking water has a pH of 7. It is considered neutral. Ocean water, however, has a pH of about 8.1. This tells us that ocean water is slightly basic. Ocean life has adapted to live in perfect balance with this pH level. But the ocean wasn't always at this pH level. Prior to the Industrial Revolution, which took place in the late eighteenth century, the pH of the ocean was about 8.2. Scientists have observed that the oceans have steadily become less basic and more acidic since the Industrial Revolution. In fact, in the past two hundred years, the ocean has become 30 percent more acidic. This increase in acidity is known as **ocean acidification**. Ocean acidification can be harmful for ocean animals and plants.

It isn't a coincidence that the Industrial Revolution triggered the ocean acidification process. The Industrial Revolution was the time when manufacturing moved from small shops to large factories, often full of newly-invented machines that consumed a lot of energy.

In the two hundred years since the start of the Industrial Revolution, human activity has increased pollution levels. This pollution is created when carbon dioxide is released into the air by driving cars, running factories, and burning fossil fuels. Carbon dioxide in the atmosphere isn't good for humans—or any of the other life on the earth. Some of this carbon dioxide is absorbed by the rain forest, but an even bigger percentage of the carbon dioxide is absorbed by the ocean. This is a really good thing for humans on land. If it weren't for oceans, the pollution problem would be far greater. The issue is, when the extra carbon dioxide in the atmosphere is absorbed by the ocean, it makes the ocean water more acidic over time.

BE THE CHANGE

The reality is, humans are producing a lot of carbon dioxide. Carbon dioxide emissions from human activity will continue to have a major impact on the health of the ocean. It's up to all of us to work together to try and lower our **carbon footprint**, which is the amount of carbon dioxide we produce every day.

Since carbon dioxide is produced by using energy, try reducing the energy you use at home. Make sure to turn off lights and appliances when you don't need them to be on. Unplug any devices and chargers when you aren't using them. Walk or bike instead of driving a car, or consider carpooling with friends.

Burning less fossil fuel for energy reduces carbon dioxide emissions and lowers the carbon footprint. Educate yourself on clean energy sources like solar and wind. Can you replace any of your outside lights that require electricity with solar-powered lights?

Small steps you take at home will have a big impact on reducing your carbon footprint. If everyone chips in to lower their carbon footprint, together we can help keep our planet healthy.

Ocean acidification is serious. Increased acid levels can destroy important coral reef habitats and break down the shells of ocean animals. Animals like oysters, clams, and crabs rely on their hard shells to keep them safe from predators. If the ocean continues to become more acidic, these animals could become endangered.

Runaway Runoff

Have you ever seen a rainbow-colored, slick-looking puddle of liquid on the pavement of a parking lot or street? That puddle is actually oil, most likely from a car. In a few days, you might return and notice that the puddle is gone. What do you think happened to that oily mess? It may have gotten absorbed into the surrounding area, seeping into the concrete or nearby soil or vegetation. Or maybe it got washed away and is dissolved somewhere nearby. The puddle may have disappeared from the parking lot, but the oil didn't magically vanish. It had to go *somewhere*.

WHAT A RACKET!

Ocean pollution isn't only about things that get dumped or absorbed into the ocean. Noise pollution is another form of ocean pollution. It is an invisible but dangerous threat to ocean animals.

Military sonar, oil drilling, cruise ships, and commercial shipping activity all produce a lot of underwater noise. These severe noise disturbances can prevent fish and whales from hearing dangers that may be around them. Noise also keeps them from finding their way, connecting with their group members, and taking care of their babies.

Wherever the oil ends up, eventually it will get picked up in runoff. (Remember when we talked about the dangers of peeing near a small body of water because that pee would eventually make its way into the lake or stream?) Runoff happens when there is more water than the ground is able to absorb. For example, imagine a heavy rainstorm. Where does all the rain go? Some of the water gets absorbed into the soil or runs into drainage or sewer systems. But sometimes there is just too much rainwater and there is no way for it to be absorbed or trapped. When this happens, the water flows across the land, streets, parking lots, and any other surfaces it can find. Remember that oil puddle that was once in the parking lot? The runoff picks up the oil particles as it flows across the surface of the parking lot. Eventually, the runoff, now laden with oil and whatever else it may have picked up along its journey, finds its way into nearby creeks, streams, or lakes. Since all water sources eventually make it to the ocean, guess where the sludge in the runoff will end up.

Sea IT FOR YOURSELF

What you'll need:

- A glass jar or container
- White vinegar
- A seashell, or eggshell if you don't have a seashell handy (eggshells are made of ingredients similar to seashells)

Place the seashell (or eggshell) into the container. Pour the white vinegar into the container so the shell is completely submerged.

Watch what happens. Can you spot tiny little bubbles fizzing on the surface of the shell? Leave the container undisturbed for 24 hours, then come back and take a look. Does the shell look any different?

What's going on here? Vinegar is an acid. The vinegar in the container breaks down the shell components. The bubbles you observe are carbon dioxide, a by-product of the breakdown process. Eventually, if you leave the shell submerged in the vinegar long enough, the shell will dissolve completely away.

Ocean acidification works the same way. When ocean water becomes more acidic, it can break down the shells of certain animals, like clams, crabs, and oysters. Without their shells to protect them, the animals' survival is threatened.

Runoff is a real problem—people are polluting the ocean without even realizing it! Some of the commonest pollutants picked up by storm water are the chemicals people use for farming, gardening, and landscaping. In order to make a lawn look green and lush, a homeowner may put down grass fertilizer. Gardens can benefit from compost, manure, and fertilizers that help flowers and vegetables grow. On large agricultural farms, crops are grown on a massive scale aided by pesticides, herbicides, and insecticides. All of these fertilizers and chemicals may be great for plants and crops, but they are often picked up by runoff and carried to the ocean, where they become pollutants.

OILY SITUATION

In 1989, a huge ship called the Exxon *Valdez* hit a reef in Prince William Sound in Alaska. The impact caused the hull of the ship to crack open, spilling more than 11 million gallons of oil into the Sound. At the time, it was the worst oil spill in history. The oil spill blanketed more than thirteen hundred miles of Alaskan coastline, killing thousands of seabirds, otters, seals, and other wildlife.

In the months that followed, thousands of workers and volunteers worked to disperse the spilled oil and rescue and clean up animals coated by it. The area has never fully recovered from the disaster.

After the accident, the United States Congress passed the Oil Pollution Act, and in 1990 it was signed into law by President George H. W. Bush. The law made stricter rules for oil tankers and imposed heavy penalties on companies which didn't follow these rules. Nobody wanted another accident like the Exxon *Valdez*. Sadly, this was not the last such oil disaster.

Polluted runoff is a threat to the health of the ocean. It's not unusual for beaches to be closed to swimming immediately after a heavy rainfall because the polluted runoff is heavily concentrated near the shore. This water isn't safe to swim in. These chemicals may help crops thrive, but they are not good for humans. Nobody wants to swim in polluted sludge. Eventually the polluted water is carried deeper out to sea, making the beachfront safe for swimming again. But, while the beach may reopen, that polluted runoff is still out there in the ocean.

Fertilizers and agricultural chemicals often contain nitrogen and phosphorus. One thing in the ocean that thrives on nitrogen and phosphorus is algae. Algae gobble these elements up, growing and reproducing in a big way, creating what is called an algal bloom. We already talked about how nitrogen and phosphorus in your pee can cause algal blooms in small bodies of water. Peeing in the ocean isn't

ALGAE

a big deal because the ocean has natural ways of handling these elements that we've already discussed. And we've already discussed how your pee is just a drop in the massive ocean. So, the nitrogen and phosphorous in your pee isn't going to trigger an algal bloom. But runoff containing fertilizers and other chemicals is much more substantial and can cause algal growth to absolutely explode. Eventually these algae die and drop to the ocean floor, where bacteria move in. The bacteria feast on the explosion of dead algae, consuming oxygen in the process. Marine life needs oxygen to survive. When enough oxygen is depleted because of the decomposing algae, a "dead zone" is formed. Very few organisms can live in a dead zone.

Dead zones can be found across both coasts of the United States and throughout the world. There are more than four hundred dead zones across the globe today, and the number of dead zones is increasing. In 2017, scientists discovered the largest dead zone in recorded history in the Gulf of Mexico. It was nearly the size of the state of New Jersey. The good news is it is possible to recover and repair a dead zone, but it takes a lot of dedication and hard work.

Drastic Plastic

Humans have become extremely dependent on a material called plastic. Plastic is everywhere. It is used in food containers, pens, toothbrushes, bottles, furniture, sports equipment, appliances, building materials, toys, electronics, packaging, and so much more. Look around you right now. You can probably spot a whole bunch of plastic items near you at this very moment.

Plastic is not a natural material—it isn't something you can grow in your backyard. It is manufactured, and there are lots of good reasons why people keep making more plastic. Plastic is flexible and easy to produce in all kinds of shapes, thicknesses, sizes, and colors. It is lightweight while being strong and durable. It's also fairly inexpensive. For all these reasons, plastic has become commonly used all across the globe.

Plastic seems pretty awesome, but plastics are a problem for the oceans, especially **single-use plastics**, which are used for only a short time and quickly discarded. An example of a single-use plastic item is a plastic shopping bag, the kind

THROUGH THE DRAINPIPES

Have you ever thought about all the waste that leaves your house? You have waste that travels away from your home from your kitchen, bathroom, and laundry. Some of that waste is liquid, like shower water. Some of the waste is more solid, like food particles, dishwashing debris, and, well . . . poop. This waste leaves your house through the plumbing. These pipes carry the waste away from your home to the street, where they are joined by other pipes leading from your neighbors' homes. All of the neighborhood waste comes together and travels through big underground pipes to a waste treatment facility. Here, the waste is cleaned and processed.

Raw sewage is wastewater that has not been treated. Raw sewage dumped into waterways creates big problems. It carries bacteria, which can lead to harmful diseases for humans and animals. Raw sewage can overrun the system, creating harmful algal blooms similar to the problems created from runoff. There are strict laws and regulations placed upon companies that manage waste treatment facilities to ensure raw sewage is handled safely and not dumped into the waterways.

you get at the store checkout to help carry your purchases. Another example of a single-use plastic is a drinking straw. After you're done with your beverage, the plastic straw is probably thrown away. What about the stuff your new toys are packaged in? When you take the toy out of its plastic packaging, that packaging probably ends up in the trash. The toy inside the packaging might be plastic, too, but it's probably not a single-use item. You're likely to play with it for a while, and maybe even give it to another kid when you're done with it so it doesn't become waste.

What's wrong with throwing away all these plastics? Plastic trash takes a really, really long time to **biodegrade,** or break down. Plastic can't decompose into nature like food scraps. Plastic takes hundreds of years to break down. There are some plastics that may never ever biodegrade. This is true for plastic that ends up in landfills as well as plastic that finds its way into the ocean. And it turns out a whole lot of

plastic makes it to the ocean. Scientists estimate that more than 9 million tons of plastic enter our ocean every year. That's the equivalent of 24 skyscrapers the size of the Empire State Building entering our oceans every year. Plastic is choking our waters.

You might be wondering how all this plastic gets into the ocean. There are a few ways this happens. Sometimes people litter. If you've ever been to the beach, you may have noticed beachgoers are not always terribly responsible with their trash. Empty water bottles, drinking straws, sunscreen tubes, food containers, and other such items are left behind as litter that gets carried away into the ocean.

Plastic litter destined for the ocean isn't only trashed at the beach. Sometimes plastic is carried to the ocean by runoff, storm drains, and even by wind. If you've ever seen a plastic shopping bag blowing in the wind, you can bet its final destination will likely be the ocean. Abandoned fishing equipment, like fishing lines and nets from large commercial fishing operations, are also contributing to the plastic problem. Plastic can even originate from the bathrooms in our homes. Some shampoos, lotions, and cosmetics contain tiny plastic particles called **microbeads** or **microplastics.** These microbeads might be good for our skin, but when they get washed down the drain and into the sewer system, eventually they end up in the ocean.

Microbeads may be tiny, but it's precisely because they are so small that they create an enormous problem. Their small size means they are easily ingested by

DESTINATION GARBAGE

There is a lot of ocean between the coast of California and Hawaii, but it's not just filled with water and marine life. There's something colossal looming in that space. It's called the Great Pacific Garbage Patch—and it's larger than the state of Texas.

The Great Pacific Garbage Patch was created by natural currents in the Pacific Ocean that carried floating plastic garbage and deposited it in one massive area. The patch is made up of all kinds of plastic items, like fishing nets and traps, plastic bottles, forks, straws, smashed-up building materials, shipping equipment, and other waste.

Scientists are looking for ways to clean up the patch, but because of its massive size this is a tricky problem to solve. To make matters worse, more and more plastic enters the ocean every day. These new pieces of trash eventually get swept into the ocean currents, finding a path to the Great Pacific Garbage Patch. This means the patch will continue to grow and grow until humans can get a handle on plastic ocean dumping.

fish. And because these plastics don't break down, they linger in the fish's body. Before long, these plastic-poisoned fish enter the human diet. In fact, in some places, microplastic is already part of the food chain.

Plastic that ends up in our oceans is extremely dangerous. Marine animals consume plastic on a regular basis. Picture a plastic bag floating through the ocean. The wavy movement of the plastic bag mimics the movement of jellyfish. A sea turtle, looking for food, could easily mistake a plastic bag for a jellyfish, its preferred food source. Rather than real food, the turtle's stomach gets filled with plastic. When this happens, the turtle can die from starvation, infection, or injury.

Sea IT FOR YOURSELF

What you'll need:

- A basin or large container
- Fresh water
- Blue food coloring (optional, but cool to simulate the color of the blue ocean)
- Small bowl
- ½ teaspoon of cocoa powder
- 2 tablespoons of cooking oil
- Mixing spoon
- Assorted absorbent materials (example: sponge, cotton balls, paper towels, newspaper scraps . . .)
- Feather

Fill the basin with water. If using blue food coloring, place a few drops into the water until the color is a bright blue. Imagine this to be your ocean water. Next, fill the small bowl with cocoa powder and cooking oil. Use the mixing spoon to combine the cocoa with the oil until it's smooth. Pour the oil solution into your ocean water. This simulates oil runoff or an oil spill.

Imagine you're an environmentalist with the tough job of cleaning up the ocean oil spill. How would you go about the cleanup? Try various strategies. You may want to dab at the oil spill with cotton balls or soak up the oil with a sponge. You may find cleaning up an oil spill isn't as easy as it looks!

Now place the feather in your oily ocean water. Imagine this is a sea bird contaminated with the oil sludge. How would you go about saving the sea bird?

FANTASTIC PLASTIC

It's true that plastics are a big problem for the ocean, but plastic, when handled properly, can be very beneficial. Plastic is used to make important medical equipment like disposable syringes, synthetic heart valves, and artificial joints. Plastics are an important component in prosthetic devices, providing flexibility, comfort, and mobility for people missing limbs. Plastics are also used in safety equipment like bike helmets, child safety seats, protective goggles, and airbags. They're also commonly used in devices important to our modern lifestyle like cellphones, computers, and televisions.

It's almost impossible to imagine a world without plastic. When used responsibly, plastic is pretty fantastic! Humans just need to be more conscientious about single-use plastic items and get in the habit of reducing, reusing, and recycling our plastic garbage.

Sometimes marine creatures get entangled in plastic. Dolphins, whales, and other sea animals can get ensnared in abandoned fishing nets. Sea birds are also often victims of plastic pollution. They are attracted to the bright color of plastic junk near the ocean's surface, mistaking it for food. Once they've eaten the plastic, they can suffocate or become very ill.

The ocean is an enormous, powerful, and essential body of water. It's hard to believe that putting something small in it, like a plastic bag or a dribble of oil, could hurt the plants and animals that call it home. But all the pollution across the planet adds up, and the ocean needs our help to stay strong and healthy. Peeing in the ocean isn't a problem. It's all the other stuff humans do that is harming the seas and, by extension, our planet.

Sea IT FOR YOURSELF

What you'll need:

- Plastic grocery bag
- Scissors
- Thread or string
- Plastic water bottle
- Water
- Blue food coloring

Flatten out the bag. Cut off the handles, then cut the bag along both sides and the bottom, so you're left with two sheets. You only need one of these sheets, so don't forget to recycle the other! Gather the center of the sheet into a small air-filled ball. Secure the ball tightly with the thread. This is the head of a jellyfish. Cut from the bottom edge up toward the head to form strips, for the jellyfish tentacles.

Fill the water bottle with water, then put your jellyfish into the bottle head first, along with a few drops of blue food coloring. Screw on the cap and shake lightly. What does it look like?

A plastic bag in the ocean looks a lot like a jellyfish, doesn't it? Some animals, like sea turtles, eat jellyfish for food. What might happen to a sea turtle who sees a plastic bag in the water and thinks it's a yummy jellyfish?

BE THE CHANGE

Small adjustments in your lifestyle can have a big impact on making the ocean healthier. If everybody does their part, we can make headway in ridding the ocean of its plastic problem.

Try finding alternatives to single-use plastic. When on the go, bring your own metal, refillable water bottle instead of a plastic one. When going to the store, carry your own reusable shopping bags. Eating out at your favorite restaurant? Skip the plastic straw. And if you have leftovers to bring home, consider using your own reusable containers rather than relying on the disposable containers from the restaurant. And always try to reuse or recycle. Familiarize yourself with your community's local recycling guidelines, so you can be sure you're only contributing items that recycling centers will actually use. Some specialty items, like electronics, can be recycled at special drop-off sites. Plastic grocery bags and other soft plastic can often be recycled at your local grocery store.

It may not seem like a lot, but even the smallest changes in our plastic usage can have a big impact on the environment.

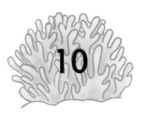

10

NOW WHAT?

By now, you probably know it's okay to pee in the ocean. Your pee won't harm the ocean. So if you're near the ocean and suddenly have the urge to pee, go for it! Everything will be just fine.

But thank you for considering the impact your actions have on the ocean. It's important to consider the effect humans have on the oceans, because if we continue down the path we're on, everything will not be just fine. While peeing isn't a problem, there are plenty of other human activities that are slowly harming the oceans. This may seem like no big deal—after all, humans live on land. Why should it matter that the ocean is hurting? Because without the oceans, we cannot have a healthy Earth. And this is YOUR planet Earth.

The Earth is more than 4.5 billion years old. That's really old! Throughout this time, Earth has been constantly changing. The continents are drifting apart. Earthquake tremors and volcanic eruptions change the landscape. Powerful forces are constantly transforming our planet and have been doing so for billions of years. Our restless Earth is never still.

But humans are changing Earth at a dangerous and harmful pace. It's up to you and all of us to take care of the world we've got. The best gift you can give your planet

BE THE CHANGE

For your next birthday, consider throwing a plastic-free birthday bash.

Decorations are an important part of any celebration. Skip the balloons and opt for plastic-free decorations. You can make personalized party banners using old fabric and some paint. Make paper chains using old newspapers that you can hang like a garland. Fresh flowers in old glass jars are always a classy touch.

Make smart, plastic-free choices when it comes to the food you serve. Ditch single-use plastic plates and utensils. Instead, use ceramic or glass plates and metal utensils which can be reused. (Yes, you should also volunteer to help your parents wash the dishes later!) Your guests will think your party is extra fancy because they get to dine using real serving ware. Or, to avoid serving ware altogether, you can serve finger foods like chicken fingers, veggies, and cheese sticks. Who wants to sit still at a party anyway? Instead of distributing plastic water bottles or juice boxes, fill a tall beverage dispenser with your favorite drink. Glass mason jars are fun to drink out of and are sturdy enough that you don't have to worry about them breaking. When the party is over you can wash out the jars and stow them away for your next party.

And don't bother with tablecloths! But if you want to cover your table, butcher paper rolls are a great choice. Throw out some crayons and let your guests doodle while they eat.

It's not that hard to throw an awesome party and skip the plastic. You'd be doing your part in protecting the planet, while wowing your friends.

is to model earth-friendly behavior. Small steps you take can have a huge impact on the oceans. Promote energy conservation. Recycle. Use eco-friendly products. Reduce your carbon footprint. Take personal responsibility for your planet. And speak up to make sure others do the same.

This may seem overwhelming. The ocean is massive, after all. Start small. Pick one small change you can make and commit to following it every day. Tell your friends and family all about your pledge and ask them to support you, maybe even join you. When you're ready, you may want to add other Earth-friendly changes to your daily routine. You may be surprised how easy it is to help the oceans. You may even find it gratifying, knowing you are saving your planet for yourself and for future generations.

AUTHOR'S NOTE

I wrote most of this book while renting a house on the ocean in the Florida Keys. It was the height of the COVID-19 pandemic, and my family was lucky enough to escape into quarantine to a secluded house on the water. I woke early every morning, grabbed a cup of coffee, and headed to the docks where a group of seabirds greeted me as the sun rose. I still remember the morning smell of the ocean. The ocean smelled different in the morning than at any other time of day, almost as if the water was bracing itself before plunging into the day. On those quiet but powerful mornings I recognized how privileged I was. What an honor to have a front row seat to earth's wonder: our oceans.

And I wrote about the beautiful ocean before me. It was easy to write this book and tell the story of the ocean because sitting on those docks, the ocean spoke to me. I remember one morning watching in awe as a school of tiny fish swam past me. There must have been thousands of these tiny fish. It was so striking to watch. I pondered where all the tiny fish were going. How did they all manage to stay together? How many fish were there? But then, something jolted me out of my wondering: a plastic bottle floating among all those tiny fish. The bottle was green and old-looking, its label long tattered and faded. How long had that plastic bottle been drifting among the fish?

The story of the ocean demanded to be told, and I am honored to tell it in this book. Our oceans are vital to the strength of our planet. It's up to all of us to keep our oceans healthy.

Dear reader, I hope one day if you are ever lucky enough to be near an ocean you will take the time to appreciate the beauty and majesty before you. Listen to the sounds of the crashing waves. Smell the ocean breeze. Gaze as far as the eye can take you and remember that the ocean needs us as much as we need it.

Ocean PROTECTOR

The ocean is Earth's most important resource, but it takes all of us to keep our oceans healthy and strong. You can be an Ocean Protector! You don't even need a fancy cape! Start by taking the Ocean Protector pledge to show you care about the ocean.

I, _____, pledge to be an Ocean Protector and work to protect the Earth's oceans from harm.

Date: _____

Signature: _____

How can you protect our oceans? Here are some ideas. Many of these actions are small and easy to take, but they can have a big impact!

- **Reduce your use of single-use plastic.** Next time you're at a restaurant, say "no, thank you" when offered a straw. Just sip directly from the glass. Bring reusable bags to the supermarket. Avoid plastic cutlery. Fill up a reusable water bottle instead of relying on single-use plastic bottles. Can you think of other single-use plastic items you can eliminate from your life?

- **Organize a neighborhood cleanup.** Litter (which is often plastic) inevitably finds its way to the ocean. Grab some friends and some garbage bags and make a fun day out of collecting litter. You'll get to hang out with friends while beautifying the neighborhood and saving the planet!

- **Use less energy.** Think of ways you might be able to reduce your energy consumption in your home. Can you commit to always turning off the lights when you leave the room? Unplugging charging cords from outlets when you're not using them? How about resolving to take shorter showers? What other ideas do you have to reduce your energy consumption?

- **Ride your bike!** If you bike to your destination instead of driving, you are reducing vehicle pollution. And as an added bonus you get some important exercise. If it's not possible to bike, look for ways to carpool.

- **Shop wisely.** Support businesses and companies that have made eco-friendly commitments. Do your research!

Ocean PROTECTOR IN ACTION!

Now it's your turn! Use the space below to write down other actions you can take to be an Ocean Protector.

_____

_____

_____

_____

_____

_____

_____

_____

_____

_____

Have you taken the Ocean Protector pledge? I'd like to hear about it! Tell me what you've pledged to do to keep our oceans healthy. Let me know at ISolvedIt@ellasbooks.com

BIBLIOGRAPHY

Fischman, Josh. "Don't Go in the Water: The Chemistry of Pee in the Pool," *Scientific American*, June 10, 2014, https://blogs.scientificamerican.com /observations/don-t-go-in-the-water-the-chemistry-of-pee-in-the-pool-video.

Geddes, Linda. "Is It Okay to Wee in the Sea?" *Telegraph*, October 16, 2018, https://www.telegraph.co.uk/travel/family-holidays/is-it-ok-to-wee-in-the -sea-science/.

Goodman, Susan E. *Gee Whiz: It's All about Pee*. New York, NY: Penguin Group, 2006.

Guy, Allison. "The Special Ingredient for Ocean Health? Animal Pee, and Lots of It," Oceana, August 17, 2017, https://oceana.org/blog/special-ingredient -ocean-health-animal-pee-and-lots-it/.

Horowitz, Kate. "Why Is Pee Yellow? (and Other Pressing Bladder Questions)," Mental Floss, March 7, 2014, http://mentalfloss.com/article/55438/why-pee -yellow-and-other-pressing-bladder-questions.

Jennings, Katie. "Is It OK to Pee in the Ocean?" *Business Insider*, August 22, 2014, http://www.businessinsider.com/is-it-ok-to-pee-in-the-ocean-2014-8 #ixzz3fSMs7JIZ.

Loeffler, John. "What Do We Do about Plastics?" Interesting Engineering, December 29, 2018, https://interestingengineering.com/what-do-we-do -about-plastics.

McNary, Sharon. "Everything You Never Wanted to Know about Pee in the Public Pool," LAist, August 17, 2018, https://laist.com/news/los-angeles-activities /everything-you-never-wanted-to-know-about-peeing-in-the-pool.

Richman, Josh and Anish Sheth, MD. *What's My Pee Telling Me?* San Francisco, CA: Chronicle Books, 2009.

Richmond, Ben. "A Spirited Endorsement of Peeing in the Ocean," *Vice*, August 23, 2014, https://www.vice.com/en/article/8qx5jp/a-spirited -endorsement-of-peeing-in-the-ocean.

Roland, James. "Is It OK to Pee in the Shower? It Depends," Healthline, March 9, 2020, https://www.healthline.com/health/shower-pee.

Serafino, Jason. "15 Things You Can Do to Help Keep Oceans Clean," Mental Floss, September 16, 2019, https://www.mentalfloss.com/article/546495/things-you -can-do-help-keep-oceans-clean.

Silverstein, Alivn, Virginia Silverstein, and Robert Silverstein. *The Excretory System*. New York, NY: Twenty-First Century Books, 1994.

Stebner, Beth. "Putting The 'P' in Pool: One in Five Adults Urinate in Swimming Pools (and It's Not the Chlorine That Makes Your Eyes Red)." *Daily Mail*, May 31, 2012, https://www.dailymail.co.uk/news/article-2152700/One-FIVE -adults-urinate-swimming-pools-70-dont-shower-diving-in.html.

Weisberger, Mindy. "How Much of the Ocean Is Whale Pee (and Worse)?" Live Science, June 21, 2017, https://www.livescience.com/55189-how-much-of -ocean-is-whale-pee.html.

Wolf, Lauren. "To Pee, Or Not To Pee? That Is the #ChemSummer Question," *Chemical & Engineering News*, July 30, 2013, http://cenblog.org/newscripts /2013/07/to-pee-or-not-to-pee-that-is-the-chemsummer-question/.

Wolf, Lauren. "What Would Happen if the Whole World Peed in the Ocean at Once?" Gizmodo, July 31, 2013, https://gizmodo.com/what-would-happen-if -the-whole-world-peed-in-the-ocean-968691464.

ACKNOWLEDGMENTS

Writing a book might feel like a solitary exercise, and while it's true that I alone must write the words, it takes an army of dedicated professionals, colleagues, friends, and family to create a book! I am deeply grateful to Megan Abbate, my fabulous editor at Bloomsbury. Megan has been a dream to work with, and I'm so lucky to have her in my corner publishing these important books. Also in my corner is the rest of the Bloomsbury team, including designer Yelena Safronova, creative director Donna Mark, copy editor Emily Goodman, managing editorial director Laura Phillips, editorial director Sarah Shumway, publishing director Mary Kate Castellani, publicist Ariana Abad, production manager Nicholas Church, and many others who worked hard to make this book happen. At a time when books are being questioned and banned across the country, Bloomsbury continues to publish the books young readers desperately need and deserve.

Thank you to Clelia Gore. *Is It Okay to Pee in the Ocean?* is my fifth published book, but the first book I ever sold. I pitched this topic to Clelia more than five years ago and she knew we were onto something here. I will forever be grateful to Clelia for launching my writing career and being my dream first agent. Thank you to Caryn Wiseman and the team at Andrea Brown for having my back and supporting the next phase of my writing journey.

A huge thank you to Lily Williams, the brilliant illustrator for this book series. The cover of this book blew me away! Somehow Lily knows the exact whimsical image a page needs to help tell the story. It has been such a joy to partner with Lily. Please check out Lily's other titles. Her books cover vitally important topics on protecting our planet.

To my family, thank you for putting up with my writing gig and supporting me on this journey. As the mother of three boys, I know a thing or two about pee. And cleaning toilets. I suppose I need to thank Harrison, Sammy, and Nate for that. To Jeff: may we travel all the oceans together. Peeing in them is optional.

To my readers, thank you for supporting my books. There is no bigger joy for an author than to hear from readers that they connected with a book. The letters, emails, and crypto solutions you've sent me propel me every day to keep charging forward. In case you're wondering . . . yes, I have peed in the ocean. I think this book has proven that peeing in the ocean is totally okay! No, I never ever pee in the pool. That's just gross. I don't pee in the shower. That's not my thing. But I do brush my teeth in the shower, which my family finds weird but seems completely normal and appropriate to me.